Wise Words

Bookish
Women

Harper *by* Design

When the world is too much, I love to read thrillers and romance novels. I just want to lose myself in something either intriguing or ludicrously romantic.

Roxane Gay

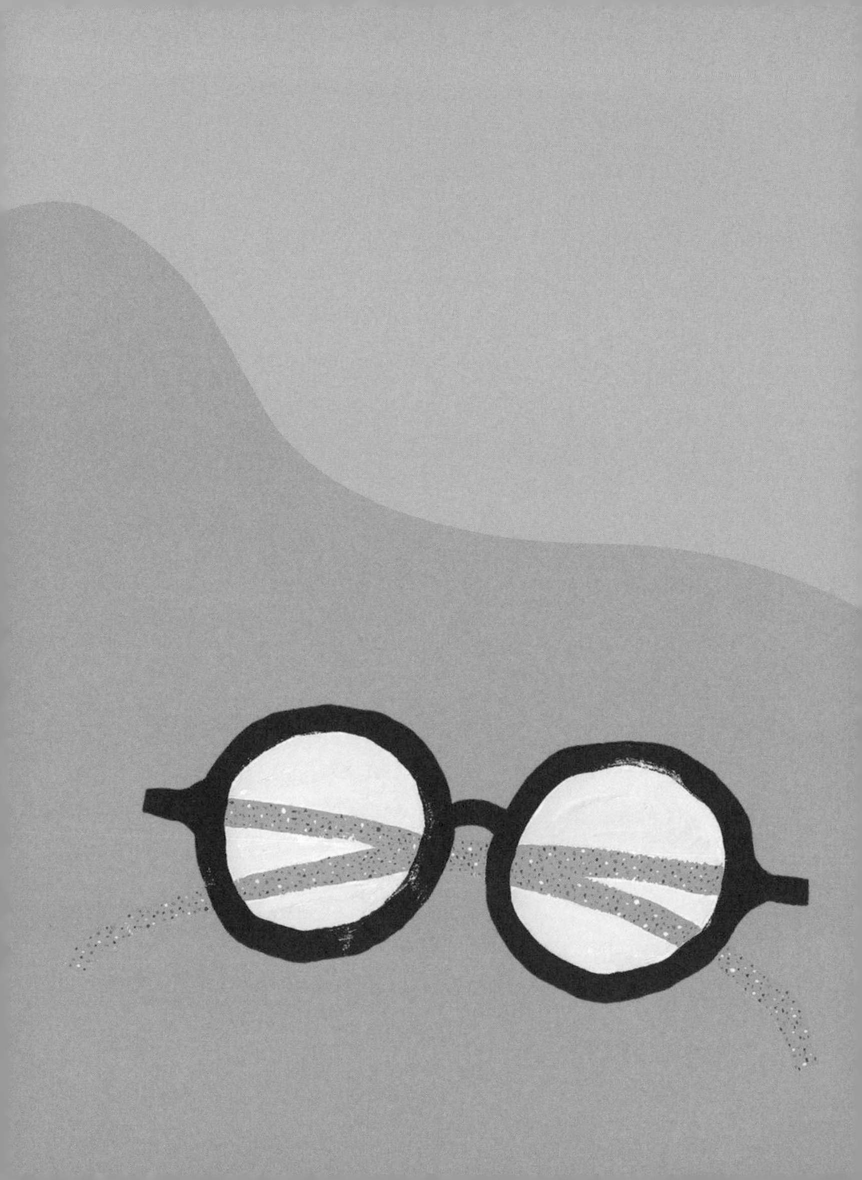

See yourself in a way
that others might
not see you, simply
because they've never
seen it before.

Kamala Harris

My mother told me
to be a lady. And for
her, that meant be
your own person,
be independent.

Ruth Bader Ginsburg

Above all, be the heroine of your life, not the victim.

Nora Ephron

The best way to be a leader – whether it's in politics, or in business, or in life – is to recognise that very few people are one dimensional.

Stacey Abrams

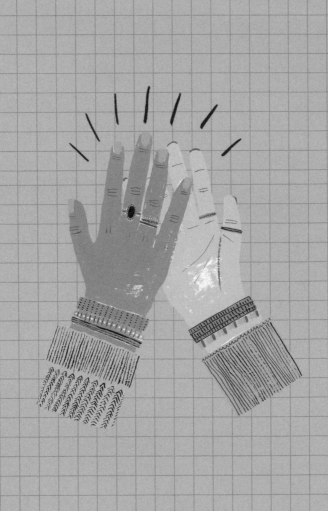

We may encounter many defeats, but we must not be defeated. In fact, it may be necessary to encounter defeats, so we can know who the hell we are.

Maya Angelou

Never listen to anyone who says you can't, or shouldn't, go on.

Hillary Clinton

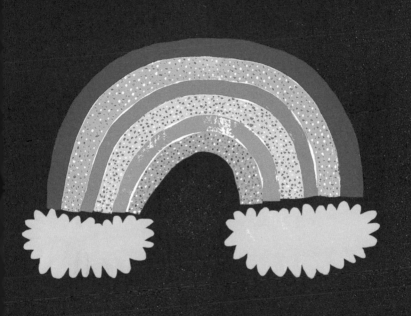

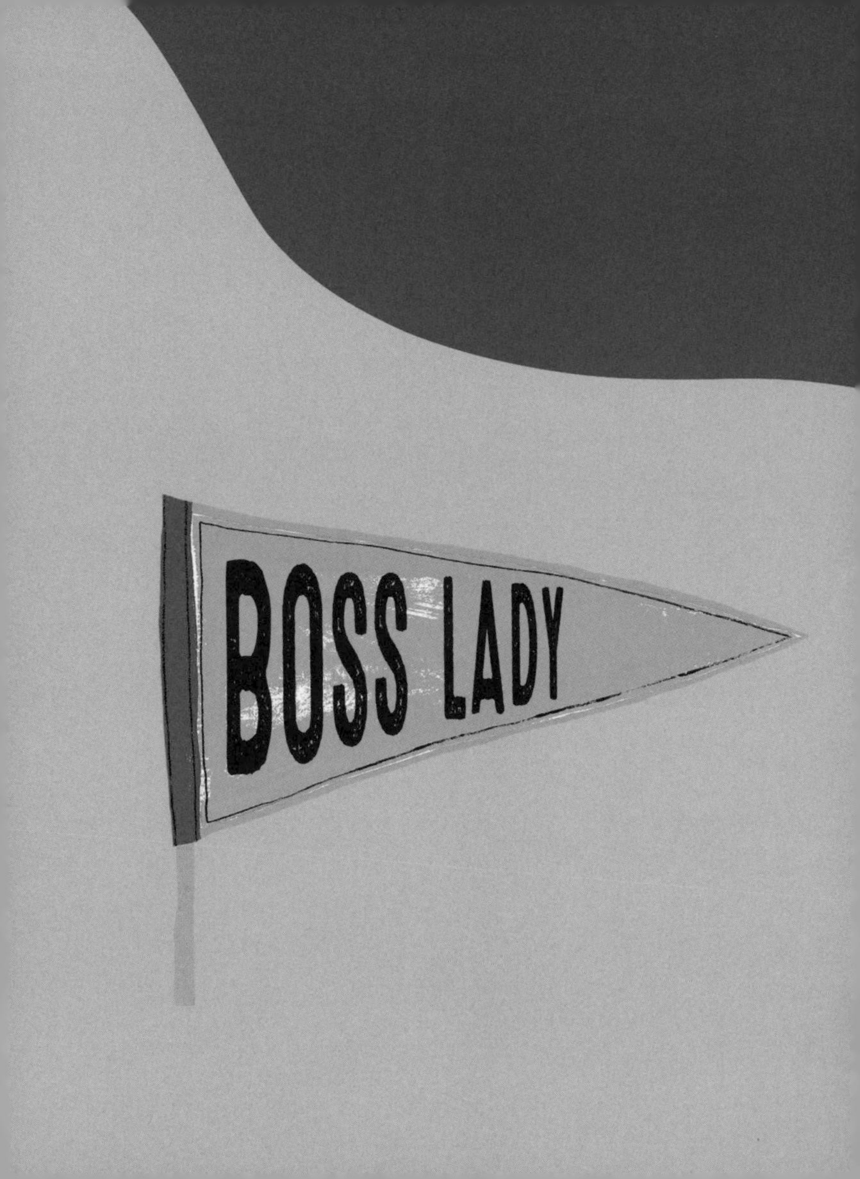
BOSS LADY

I encourage women to step up. Don't wait for somebody to ask you.

Reese Witherspoon

It took me quite a long
time to develop a voice,
and now that I have it,
I am not going to
be silent.

Madeleine Albright

Fill your mind with knowledge – it's the only kind of power no one can take away from you.

Min Jin Lee

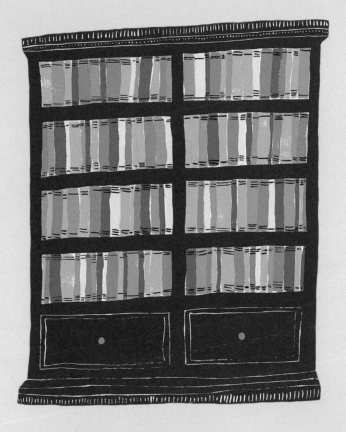

If you sit and wait to feel like you are the most confident person in the room, you are probably going to be left by yourself.

Jacinda Ardern

You wanna fly, you got
to give up the shit that
weighs you down.

Toni Morrison

Anger has a long
history of bringing
about positive change.

**Chimamanda
Ngozi Adichie**

One child, one teacher, one book, one pen can change the world.

Malala Yousafzai

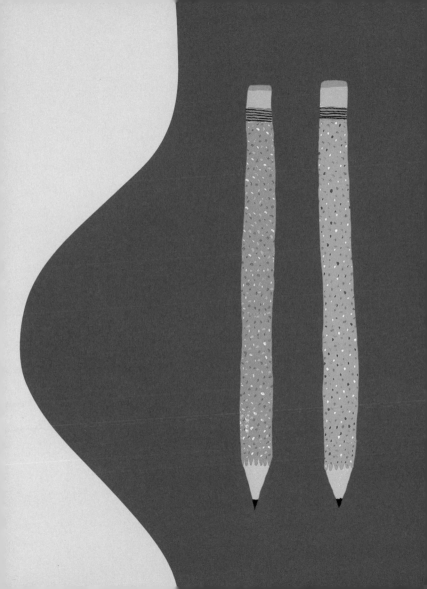

People who read are
people who dream,
and we connect through
the stories we live and
tell and read.

Amy Poehler

A lot of people like to ask me, 'How on earth do you balance family and career?' Men never get asked that question. Because they don't.

Ali Wong

That's what great books do, especially when shared. They shine a light on the unfolding of our own stories.

Oprah Winfrey

Fear has never been a good adviser, neither in our personal lives nor in our society. Cultures and societies that are shaped by fear will without doubt not get a grip on the future.

Angela Merkel

Libraries are reservoirs of strength, grace and wit, reminders of order, calm and continuity, lakes of mental energy, neither warm nor cold, light nor dark.

Germaine Greer

When girls are educated, their countries become stronger and more prosperous.

Michelle Obama

I've come to believe that amongst all the good human qualities, there is none greater than kindness.

Leigh Sales

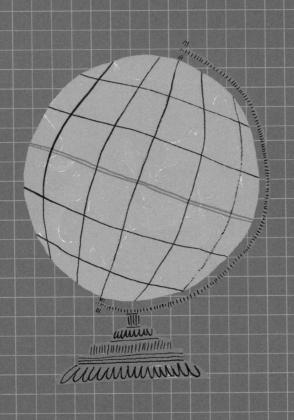

A truly equal world
would be one where
women ran half
our countries and
companies, and men
ran half our homes.

Sheryl Sandberg

If you want something said, ask a man; if you want something done, ask a woman.

Margaret Thatcher

My idea of good company is the company of clever, well-informed people who have a great deal of conversation; that is what I call good company.

Jane Austen

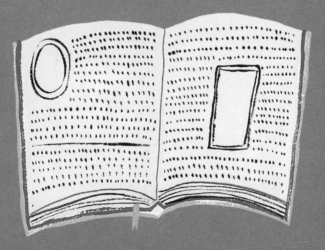

I know reform is
never easy. But I know
reform is right.

Julia Gillard

Change is opportunity
in disguise.

Erin Brockovich

Making a damn
fool of yourself is
absolutely essential.

Gloria Steinem

You can choose not to
be interested in politics,
but you can't choose
to be unaffected by it.

Penny Wong

A place belongs
forever to whoever
claims it hardest.

Joan Didion

The internet isn't reality. The things people are typing are words in an app you can choose to ignore. Put your phone down, close your eyes, count to 10. Think about how you can make the world a better place in the real world. We need you out here.

Lizzo

I'm not much of a cook.
I used to keep books
in my gas oven – until
someone told me it was
a fire hazard.

Michiko Kakutani

You're not an avocado.
Not everyone's going
to love you.

Liz Cambage

Be brave and be kind
because you will always
get stronger by the path
you leave behind.

Nakkiah Lui

Great people talk about ideas, average people talk about things, and small people talk about wine.

Fran Lebowitz

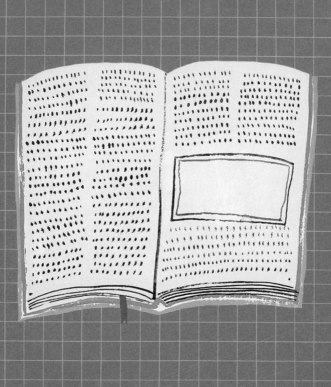

I remember watching Margaret Cho with my grandmother on TV. She was my hero, not only because she was funny, but because she showed me that it's okay to be yourself, that it's okay to be a brash yellow girl and to be a strong and brave woman.

Awkwafina

I'm curious about
everything, except
what people have
to say about me.

Sarah Jessica Parker

When you put love out in the world it travels, and it can touch people and reach people in ways that we never even expected.

Laverne Cox

Nothing is absolute.
Everything changes,
everything moves,
everything revolves,
everything flies
and goes away.

Frida Kahlo

Say yes, and you'll figure it out later.

Tina Fey

If someone really wants to see you, they always find a way. Always.

Mindy Kaling

I really think a champion is defined not by their wins but by how they can recover when they fall.

Serena Williams

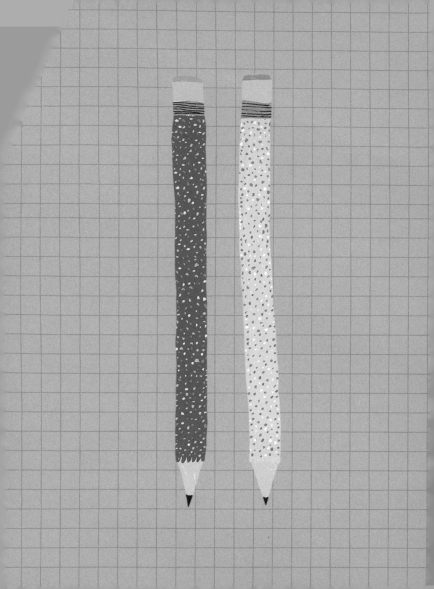

It's a sign of your own worth sometimes if you are hated by the right people.

Miles Franklin

If you feel rooted
in your home and
family, if you're active
in your community,
there's nothing more
empowering. The best
way to make a difference
in the world is to start by
making a difference in
your own life.

Julia Louis-Dreyfus

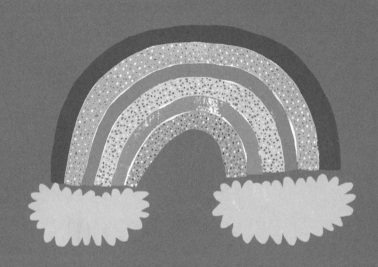

You are never too small
to make a difference.

Greta Thunberg

Writing is part
intuition and part trial
and error, but mostly
it's very hard work.

Cheryl Strayed

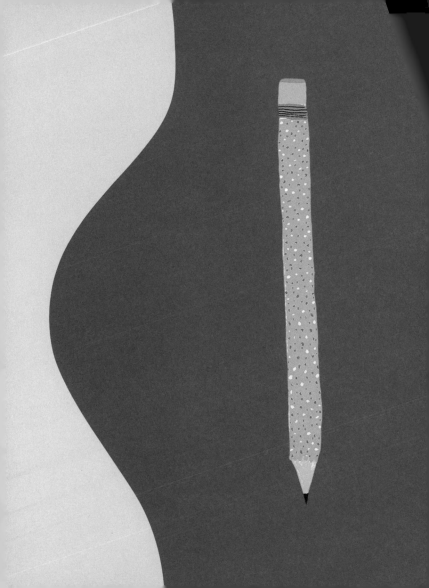

Nobody's happy all the time. But I work hard at it.

Dolly Parton

Mentors of mine were under a big pressure to minimise their femininity to make it. I'm not going to do that. That takes away my power. I'm not going to compromise who I am.

Alexandria Ocasio-Cortez

Harper *by* Design
An imprint of HarperCollins*Publishers*

HarperCollins*Publishers*
Australia • Brazil • Canada • France • Germany • Holland • Hungary
India • Italy • Japan • Mexico • New Zealand • Poland • Spain • Sweden
Switzerland • United Kingdom • United States of America

First published in Australia in 2022
by HarperCollins*Publishers* Australia Pty Limited
Level 13, 201 Elizabeth Street, Sydney NSW 2000
ABN 36 009 913 517
harpercollins.com.au

Design and compilation copyright © HarperCollins*Publishers* Australia Pty Limited 2022

This work is copyright. Apart from any use as permitted under the *Copyright Act 1968*,
no part may be reproduced, copied, scanned, stored in a retrieval system, recorded,
or transmitted, in any form or by any means, without the prior written permission of the publisher.

A catalogue record for this book is available from the National Library of Australia

ISBN 978 1 4607 6062 8

Publisher: Mark Campbell
Publishing Director: Brigitta Doyle
Designer: Mietta Yans, HarperCollins Design Studio
Illustrator: Nicole Cicak
Printed and bound in China by RR Donnelley

8 7 6 5 4 3 2   23 24 25